Here for the Music

poems by
Laurie Brinklow

Text © 2012 by Laurie Brinklow

All rights reserved. No part of this publication may be reproduced, stored in a retrieval system, or transmitted, in any form or by any means, without the prior written permission of the publisher or, in case of photocopying or other reprographic copying, a licence from the Canadian Copyright Licensing Agency.

ACORNPRESS

P.O. Box 22024
Charlottetown, Prince Edward Island
C1A 9J2
acornpresscanada.com

Design by Matt Reid
Cover art by Pamela Swainson
Editing by Jane Ledwell
Printed and bound in Canada

Library and Archives Canada Cataloguing in Publication

Brinklow, Laurie
Here for the music / Laurie Brinklow.

Poems.
ISBN 978-1-894838-82-5

I. Title.

PS8553.R5335H47 2012   C811'.6   C2012-905668-5

Canada   Canada Council for the Arts   Conseil des Arts du Canada

The publisher acknowledges the support of the Government of Canada through the Canada Book Fund of the Department of Canadian Heritage for our publishing activities. We also acknowledge the support of the Canada Council for the Arts for our publishing program.

For my mom,
Mary Lou Rowbotham,
who has believed in the music since the beginning,
and my daughters,
Heather Cowan and Mikhala Brinklow-McKnight,
who keep me singing

Contents

Leavin's Just Another Word

Pile Driver	2
Tidal Waves	4
The Queen of Prince Rupert	5
Saskatchewan Time	6
Highway 11	7
Scars	8
Mrs. Ashby	9
When Greggy Drowned	10
Ravishing Ruby	11
Hope Chest	12
A Place for Everything	13
Prince George	14
Yellowhead	15
Card Shark	16
Sweet Sixteen	17
First Degree of Separation	18

Swimming Lessons

First Time	20
Once a Month the Egg Travels	21
Moons	23
Delivery Room	24
Swimming Lesson	25
When the Tooth Fairy Forgets	26
Hair	27
Since I'm 37	28

Sculpture	29
Either/Or	30
Wanted Words	31
Sometimes When I Sleep	32
We Have Fallen	34
Willow	35
Feet	36
One by One	37
For Linda	41
Eleanor's Eyes	43
If I Could Draw	44
Choir	46
Sleeping	47
What the Apple Lady Sees	48
Dust	50
On Learning Someone You Know Is Having an Affair	51
Seven-year-itch	52
Cold Feet	53
A Threat or a Promise?	54
"Boys Like Girls Whose Hair Outweighs Their Brain"	55
Eight and Counting	58
Blue Moon	59
Out of Wedlock	60

Living at Sea Level

The Language of Seashells	63
Living at Sea Level	65
Biding Your Time	73

Leavin's Just Another Word

Pile Driver

High on your throne
in the river, waters part
pile driver
pounds

Cross-country pilgrim to the land of promise with
three kids under five, the wife, green '57 Chev –
go west, Canadian cowboy, your dreams
in the pages of Louis L'Amour

levers rhyme
gears grind
dead weight
pounds

Crying, Mom screams
now what will we do – no cheque –
how could you just lose it?
You shrug your shoulders
close your eyes, hide the steel
blue
Later finds out
you lost it
in a poker game

Up before dawn
home after dark
ten- and twelve- and twenty-one-hour days
You come home
have your supper, a beer
then another
few words
then bed
The trailer rocks to your beat

We watch
as you slave
fat overtime cheques and barmaids
drive you to
shovels, backhoes and cranes
Five thousand work hours in one year alone
a fine operator, the best
Hell of a guy

I see you
rounded back hunched
bottle on the breakfast table
your fist comes down
and we run

Tidal Waves

In 1964 we lived in the hills of Northern British Columbia, far enough away from the tidal wave that filled the swimming pool of the Vancouver Island motel where we moved a month after with logs and black sea from a wave that began in Alaska and ended twelve hundred miles to the Pacific south.

It was winter and I was six and I longed for summer and to swim in a pool just outside my front door, if only the motel owner would please clean it out. But instead it sat black, so I thought about that wave, how it had gone halfway to my aunt's house three miles from the ocean, *look, that's where it stopped, that tree right there,* and I dreamed of green mountain slopes, lush with trees that grew right up to the sky.

All spring we picked golf balls for fifty cents a bucket with my mom after school and on Saturdays from the driving range behind the motel, the grass a flat green sponge. Then I got the measles and had to stay inside for two weeks with the curtains pulled, the fear of going blind if I looked knotted in my belly. And I'd shrink when I'd hear them talk through the walls, *Vancouver Island is going to sink, you know...*

In June they cleaned out the pool and I swam in the new water maybe twice before we moved up-Island to another new job and the second time I remember I almost drowned when my hand slipped off the edge I couldn't touch the bottom water went up my nose all I could see was bubbles—

For six weeks that summer we lived in another motel with no pool before the talk of Vancouver Island sinking made us leave for good. Or maybe it was just that my dad got a new job. And it just happened to be in a safe and high place where trees began and never ended.

The Queen of Prince Rupert

It rained the year we lived in Prince Rupert, grey sky blending to ocean to photographs of a house on Water Street, a white cat named Frosty who slept in the bathroom sink, and me looking like all the other little girls at my eighth birthday party.

My father built the new pulp mill, while I got to wear a Catholic dress to a Catholic school and we weren't even Catholic.

My mother was eight-and-a-half-months pregnant when my Ontario grandmother died, so we couldn't go to the funeral. I learned how to knit and my mom fell taking the cat to the vet. She hit her belly and her chin and told everyone that that was why the baby had such a flat nose. I got to name my golden-haired sister Angela after the cousin of the first boy I ever kissed in a tent under the table on the front porch.

Mornings I'd climb down stairs from the attic bedroom I shared with my brother, where I learned to sleep with covers to my chin, skeletons in every cupboard and a guillotine above my head. My sister slept in a car bed on the floor beside my parents and my dad rocked her with his foot when she cried.

There was another picture: my dad standing between the man he worked for and the man-he-worked-for's wife. Her name was Donna, and she was who he was with while we waited in line for the *Queen of Prince Rupert* so we wouldn't have to drive a thousand miles to my dad's new job. I remember my mother moved our yellow station wagon out of the line, and told them to tow away my dad's red pick-up while the parking lot emptied around us into the boat. And I remember sleeping on the floor of a motel, and my mother nursing Angela, while rain spattered the window.

He showed up two days later in time for the next boat and had a toothache the whole trip while I threw up all the way to Vancouver Island.

Saskatchewan Time

Six a.m. Summer and we're in a grain field, not far from the long black stain the pipeline has smeared across the plain. My parents are on the table that folds down in the front. I am in the bottom bunk, ten feet away. I am stuck in a dream but I still hear their waking: dad to go to work, mom to turn over and go back to sleep as soon as he leaves. They're not fighting. The sun is a fireball perched on the edge of the world.

I get out of bed and I go to them. My stomach hurts and I'm crying. I tell them I'm the tiniest creature and I'm shrinking I'm sinking the world has become outer space it's so huge I'm so small I reach out to touch my brother above me I can't feel or see my arm, my fingers, I'm falling. But not moving. The key is going to get me the key is going to get me the key—

It's okay, they say, nothing is going to get you, we're here, you're here, right here, go back to bed, it's early. Daddy has to go work, now go back to bed.

I crawl back in, but now I'm awake, back turned to their morning, and once more I'm sinking, falling. I can hear my dad putting on his coveralls, going into the bathroom, toilet seat hitting the wall. My mother pulls a housecoat from the heap on the floor, static crackles. She turns on the water, fills the kettle. The sun hangs.

I still have that dream every now and again, just on the edge of sleep, I become a dot on the prairie landscape. I reach out to stars and I cannot see my hand.

Highway 11

September in Huntsville, Northern Ontario, and our trailer is parked in the campground out by Highway 11. We are a village of nomads, building the gas pipeline from Bracebridge to Geraldton. I am thirteen.

It's a perfect Indian summer afternoon, and I'm back in the woods, wading in the stream. I'm thinking the most wonderful thing to do right now would be to float down it on my back, sun dancing on the water like kids who for a few minutes forget about school and homework and winter coming.

September, and there are only a few days like this, where just taking off your clothes and jumping in would make the difference between remembering and not remembering. Instead, I run home for my bathing suit, past the cabin where the man who taught me how to play chess lives, through the woods where I long for Terry Rossbottom whose dad has the Esso on the corner to lay me down on the moss and kiss me, that first uncertain kiss, through the campground where we play hide-and-seek every night, to our trailer where the floor of the bathroom is also the shower and my brother sleeps in the top bunk and my parents on the table. I jump into my bathing suit, rummage through the cupboard for a towel. By the time I get back, the sun is gone and the water's cold, just another stream in the woods.

We move, but whenever we drive by on our way to Toronto, I stick my head out the window to see the house where Terry Rossbottom lives, or maybe spot him pumping gas. And we cross the bridge over the stream, and I see me floating there on my back, body open to the sun.

Years later I still look. The house and gas station are gone, and the highway is so sprawled across the moss that there isn't a bridge anymore, just a culvert for the spring run-off and a trickle in the fall.

Scars

Daddy rolled cars like the cigarettes he let me eat in the park when I was one. One time it was on the radio how Mom found out, cooking supper. She sat, dead weight like the iron frying pan she threw at him when I was three. It hit the wall.

Later he'd drive up in a borrowed pick-up, turban wound around his head, stitches on his hands and arms, raggedy grin on his face. She'd open the door, let him in.

The year my brother drowned, it was our trailer ended up at the bottom of a mountain, moving us from Dawson Creek to Vancouver Island. Pieces of our lives strewn like garbage in a dump. Salvaged a couple of seconds' worth, like the picture of me that proved I was the prettiest baby in all of Peterborough (*don't let her hear, it'll go to her head*). She got twenty-five dollars and the picture in a frame, bought matching outfits for me and my brother. She buried him in his.

My arm forever scarred from where the glass broke, though the smile is still there. In my living room now it hangs between my daughters, at one, at two, at four. I check their arms. For scars.

Mrs. Ashby

Grade 4 and Mrs. Ashby is my favourite teacher in the whole world. She's younger than my mom and prettier than my mom and she plays games and doesn't yell when I take too long to look up words in the dictionary because I get distracted by all the other words around them.

We're in our travel trailer in the trailer court in Skookumchuck, where my dad is building the pulp mill on the other side of the river. Every morning I get up at quarter to seven to ride the bus twenty-seven miles to school in Kimberley. I do my math homework and social studies homework and read books and brush the rats' nests out of my hair, and in winter I make little baby feet walk up the frosty windows with my sideways fist and fingers.

Mrs. Ashby knows I love music, because I always go to the music room and play the piano when my work is finished. I play the melodies I hear on the radio and sometimes pretend I'm playing with two hands like Liberace on my aunt's TV, feel fingers connect to the keys which hit the strings which make the notes bounce like pingpong balls off the back of the piano. Sometimes it sounds like thunder and a grown-up yelling and sometimes like rain on our trailer roof. Sometimes it sounds like my cat Ivory's purr and sometimes like somebody crying.

In June the pulp mill is finished, so I tell Mrs. Ashby we're moving again. On the last day of school Mrs. Ashby says in front of the whole class that she has a special prize for me, something she knows I want more than anything in the whole world. A piano. I wonder if she's asked my parents, if she knows we live in a trailer and there isn't room for a piano. She says come and get your prize, and I think it must be in the music room because I don't see it beside her desk. I walk toward the door, and she says, no here, and holds out her hand. A plastic box. Stuck in a red sponge. A tiny gold pin shaped like a piano.

My face gets stuck. My words get stuck, too, and I mumble and follow my toes back to my desk. I sit on my hands all the way home on the bus, my piano in my pocket.

When Greggy Drowned

He took the glint from Daddy's eye, leaving little for the other son, four-eyed sissy who Mom said cried whenever a fly landed on his arm, smallest in the class, the one the dogs and big boys chased.

I was lost in books while he went to hockey camp and 6 a.m. practices, never fast enough, never good enough for the father who tried to find himself in bottles of Silent Sam stashed behind the Arctic Cat my brother broke then dissected on the basement floor. *Couldn't tell his ass from a hole in the ground,* Daddy'd say to anyone who'd come visit.

Later, when my sister came, brother would poke and tease her til I'd chase him down the hallway of our trailer, round the cedar chest to the corner between the closet and the bed, pound his back til my fury turned to screams I couldn't tell were mine or his. Or he'd taunt, *You have bad breath.* I'd say, *I wish you were the one who drowned.*

Now, driving me home from university, slouched against the door, arm curled around the wheel like our dad, I ask him if he remembers. He says no. *I'm sorry anyway.* Shrugs. Misses his sister's wedding, his daughter's first Christmas. Has to work.

Ravishing Ruby

She was a red half-ton Ford, *Ravishing Ruby* on a sign mounted like a stallion on the hood. You could spot her coming a mile away. Held a wife and three kids when she wasn't driving to work or parked between the doors that said *Beer Parlour* and *Ladies and Escorts*. And sometimes she did then, too, hot days when he'd go for just one and we'd sit and wait and cry and fight and wish we had a different dad.

I slept the sleep of a pup wrapped on Ruby's floor, ten years old and my brother eight and my sister two, wrapped round my mother's feet driving from Skookumchuck to Lloydminster to visit Auntie Donna and Uncle Terry for Christmas. We drove all night, his cigarettes and Lynn Anderson singing "Rose Garden" lulled me to sleep. Moonlight shimmering through the frosty glass where we'd made peepholes with our breath. Their trailer stuffy and hot as we piled into bunkbeds, while they drank Seagram's V.O. and played euchre into the night.

When I was old enough, he tried to teach me to drive her. Three-foot-long gear shift with the black ball on top. Nearly blew the engine when I shifted from third to second barrelling down a hill. Later when he'd forgiven me he told me about why you shouldn't drink and drive, the empties could roll under the brake pedal. And couldn't I put my shoes the hell on.

One summer Ruby hit a moose, me home from school and my summer job pilot-car driver. On our way to Jasper to pick up a trailer, I was about a mile behind him, Mount Robson a sleeping dog on my left, crackle from the CB radio my lifeline, the air suddenly went dead. Came up from behind, outline of the moose on the shoulder of the road. Ruby lost her mirror and a strip of chrome, game warden filled his freezer. That night Daddy bought me my first legal beer in the bar in Jasper. We talked about near misses and the drivers who'd been killed and how our next-door neighbour Tete almost lost Nana when she hit a moose, in hospital for months.

Now he passes his days building models and drinking beer in his ninth-floor apartment where he lives with a woman I've never met, Ruby long gone.

Painting *Ruby* in tiny red letters on hoods and wings and keels.

Hope Chest

My mother's hope chest always sat at the foot of my parents' bed. When I was twelve I learned how to open it: silken blond veneer concealed a red cedar heart. Ran hands over wood, closed my eyes, breathed Vancouver Island green.

There I found a compartment of a mother's life: blue baby sweater, first pair of shoes, Yogi Bear piggy bank, a boxful of sympathy cards, newspaper clippings and an obituary for a green-eyed child. *Greggy drowned in the bathtub, Greggy drowned in a glass of water.*

Greggy was playing too close to the edge one spring and fell into the creek dressed in his snowsuit. The newspaper said the current carried him six miles in two hours before he was finally stopped. *Greggy drowned in the bathtub, Greggy drowned in a glass of water.*

He was two and I was five, and my parents were eight hundred miles south and I remember they flew home right away but not fast enough to save us.

My mother lives alone in an apartment now. Her hope chest sits beside my bed. My daughter asks, *What's in there, Mom?* Blankets, I tell her, just blankets.

A Place for Everything

Burnt-coffee air, soot-silt snow, Kapuskasing a brief smudge on the line of steel my father is laying across Northern Ontario. It's April and I'm in my fourth school since September, five of us in our eighteen-and-a-half-foot trailer, mama cat, five kittens, dog. Books and Scrabble and sleep the only curtain that keeps out words like money and booze and leaving you.

Finally she does. Wednesday, June fourth, just before my best friend Barb's birthday. I can't remember finding her gone, or who watched my little sister, or who made lunch and supper or who washed the dishes. Don't remember anyone asking, *Where's Mom?* I do remember she took the dog.

Thursday. Friday. Saturday. I go to Barb's for a sleepover, instead we don't sleep, watch horror shows on TV til someone says let's watch the sun come up, drag sleeping bags to the back stoop, then go quiet as blue-bruise sky flattens to steel grey, trees start to loom and grow shadows and long secrets, steal dreams. Seven a.m. and my watch must be wrong, the others sleeping and the sky's cold ash, no colour, no sound. Sunday and the sun's abandoned me.

I go in, wish Mom would pick me up, but it's Dad. Don't remember asking if he's heard from her, or him saying her name. I watch my face looking out the truck window as we drive the empty road home.

Monday. Tuesday. Wednesday. Thursday home from school and there she is. She has a new home, twenty-seven-foot Golden Falcon she saw on her way back, with a pull-out couch so they won't have to sleep on the table anymore, a bathroom with a bathtub, and a bedroom in the back. For us. Nothing said, no, *How are you*, no, *I missed you so much*, no, *Sorry I left*, not to us anyway. And in the new trailer with the bedroom with the door, we couldn't have heard if she had.

Prince George

A trailer park on the other side of the tracks where boys impatient to get anywhere dare each other to roll under the trains between shudders of coupling and uncoupling, learning young that timing is everything.

Two miles from school to home, kicking the same rock to make the walk go faster, and there's Uncle Mike with my dad at the kitchen table full of beer bottles and ashtrays, their shadows shrouded in smoke. Not really our uncle, but we've called him that since we were little, in Dawson Creek, where we used to live. He's hauling the mail from Vancouver, decided to break his trip halfway. We make ourselves scarce, to our homework and library books, stray strands of voices and the stink of stale beer seep under our doors.

Bedtime and they're still at it, Seagram's now and they're getting blurry, tongues fat as Mrs. Busby's dachshund in the trailer across the road, and through the walls laughter careens, ice cracks, liquid swishes as more rye's poured.

Then quiet, scary quiet. Something I've not heard before. The sound of a man crying.

How can he ever forgive himself, or Auntie Annika, for trusting a two-and-a-half-year-old to stay away from the spring creek at the end of the road, or his own kids for running home, singing *Greggy's gone swimming, Greggy's gone swimming,* or his own kids for living.

Greggy, the child who ate a whole package of chocolate ex-lax, the child who fell into the septic tank, the child who'd look you in the eye as he'd pick up our mother's favourite green glass ashtray and drop it, laughing. Greggy the magic child, Greggy the push-the-limits child, see Auntie Annika running, frantic, *this can't be happening, if I just close my eyes and open them again he'll be here, laughing, laughing.*

Uncle Mike stops crying, I hear the front door close, his truck shatter stillness. I don't hear my father go to bed. In the morning, all the ashtrays full, the bottles empty.

Yellowhead

I'm in the back seat of our '63 Chev sedan, driving west on the Yellowhead, between Tete Jean Cache and McBride. My two-year-old sister's asleep beside me on the seat, dog nestled up against the balloon of her bum. Heat like water vapours over asphalt and we're washing through ocean waves of rape seed, liquid sun, Mount Robson behind us on the right, more just like it on the left, and either side are fields sketched out with weathered grey logs hitched together like accidents.

I'm ten, my brother is eight, and he's in the front seat because we had a fight in Jasper two hours ago. He wanted another turn and of course he won because he started to cry. And now he's asleep and I'm in the back fit to be tied because all I can see are bright yellow rectangles on either side and an upside-down black triangle out the front where the road eels to the west.

Later we'll stop for gas, and I'll take the dog for a pee, dry brown grass cutting into cracked brown feet. My mother will buy us salt-and-vinegar chips and Orange Crush from the silver cooler under the Texaco sign. We won't talk about how she left my dad in Saskatchewan, slamming the trunk on words we block out, fingers in ears, and that she's been driving for eighteen hours and there's still five to go before we're home. She won't say how just a bit further ahead is sure to be the black-green relief of forest, because right now it's all road and heat and sweat crawling between shoulder blades, her legs stuck to the seat.

Card Shark

It's Christmas, day five of a twenty-four-hour flu, and I can barely get out of bed, let alone play Crazy 8s for the 259th time with my six-year-old. *C'mon, Mommy, play with me*, and I say, *I'm too sick*, and she starts to cry. *Okay, okay*, I say, *but let's play something else. Crazy 8s is driving me crazy.* So I teach her rummy. And gin. Blackjack. Scat. With nickels. I even try poker but I can't remember if a full house beats a straight flush. Then the fever takes over.

I'm back with my grandpa, bottle of rye at his elbow, legs crossed right over left so far the right foot touches the floor like he's walking, hand-rolled cigarette dangling from his lips and I shiver when I see the little brown hairs coming out the end catch fire. *31*, he grunts and pushes to his pile another of the nickels I stole from the change on the table in the room where my parents are sleeping. Winks at me as, mad, I throw down the cards. Then, *C'mon, Grandpa, let's play some more.* Later it's Cheat with the cousins in the rec room, while upstairs at the kitchen table you can't see the aunts and uncles for the cigarette smoke. Euchre again, which nobody plays out west, but home for Christmas in Ontario and that's how they catch up on Uncle Alvin's heart attack and you know Lyola was going to give her baby to Bernard and Lou to bring up but then she changed her mind, and did you hear about Timmy, ran into a barbed wire fence on his ski-doo, only thirteen you know. What'd you say trump was?

And my grandmother's in the living room, lips prim and tea cup perched atop her massive breasts, Jesus on the cross looking over her left shoulder, and I remember hearing how Grandpa dropped her and the ten kids off to church on Sundays on his way to the bootlegger, and how she made my Dad swear on the bible at fifteen that he'd never drink or date girls. Grandma still hates my mother, sends her clippings from Ann Landers about the ungrateful daughter-in-law.

But the picture I like best was a few years later, Dad picking them up from the train for Christmas, four hours in the pick-up passing the rye, Grandma in the middle taking a sip each time the bottle goes by. Me waiting at home, nickels at the ready.

Sweet Sixteen

And oh, I'd been kissed, too many times to tell the new boy with the Bee Gee curls and the Aussie voice, whose parents sent him to Canada when they caught him smoking dope.

Out of the frying pan into two weeks of Penticton sun, where if the world ends the sprinklers will still spew water onto luscious soil, liquid dark, oak-leaf skies, all hands and mouths and arms and legs, heady breeze pets our skin naked-dry, but we stop just in time, gasping—

Mornings he skips pottery, sneaks into the church where I'm waltzing Chopin with two left hands, kisses me on the piano bench then does the "Crocodile Rock", I sing "Daniel" and "Annie's Song" and we kiss some more.

Afternoons we skip and shout our way down Main Street to the lake where we read Ayn Rand out loud, rub oil all over and push each other off the dock, suppertime, take turns pulling one another up Main Street, hot-tired, but never too tired for night.

Twenty-two years I keep the vase he made under my piano, dried flowers crumble and fall but now he's in my living room, telling me how he looked up my name in the Vancouver phone book and found me on this island on the other side of the country, how I left my handprints when the clay was wet.

I empty the vase and fill it with acorns and lake water, whisper *Daniel*, wait for night.

First Degree of Separation

I cut my teeth on three-chord songs, steel bar of Dad's Hawaiian guitar offering a degree of separation between fingers and strings, sliding like ice cubes on a frozen pond or fingernails on a blackboard, depending on the time of night. Wilf and Hank and Johnny different every time he sings them, lines messed up or verses missing or just dee-dee-dee, stubby at his feet.

"Freedom's just another word for nothing left to lose" my first chorus, age ten and his arms hug me from behind, sweat and beer and Brylcream up my nose. Axle-grease-stained fingers squeeze mine as we grip the pick, guide the bar up and down the neck. He tells me it's tuned to C major, and firsts and fourths and fifths all the chords I'll ever need as la'n-dee-da-dee-da fills the spaces between us.

I'm thirteen when I notice we don't play like Glen Campbell on TV. His fingers move with lives of their own, fingertips kiss strings, he plays notes as well as chords, and I hear firsts and fourths and fifths, and some my dad didn't tell me about. But I recognize sad when I hear it.

B&B Music Store happy to part me from my babysitting money. Home with a real guitar and songbooks, chord charts with their suspended sevenths and augmented fifths, and minors, but the strings cut my fingers so I put it away, go back to playing my dad's.

But my songs now have holes where I know the sad goes.

Swimming Lessons

First Time

Nechako Lake tastes gun-metal grey as I paddle round the point. Spray sheens my face, clothes leaden with lake.

The man in the cottage pulls me in. I'm eighteen and he's thirty, a friend of my father's, but I know intent when I see it, magnetic north, though the Baby Duck he gives me blurs my impressions like the hard plastic truck seat crisscrossing my back and buttocks and legs.

He drives me home.

Grime and grit of oily dirt and the smoke of his cigarettes catch in my hair, air freshener cloys, and the iron taste in my mouth is the blood that stains memory.

Once a Month the Egg Travels

Six-week check-up
ask if there's anything new
in the birth control department

Gives me a pamphlet
the one the teenagers get
Grade 8: *Take it home and show your mother*
Hide it in my underwear drawer
so my brother and sister won't see

Still the same, mostly
IUD, diaphragm, condoms and foam, the Pill
rhythm—that old stand-by—
and bio-therm, the new improved version

but *not* breast-feeding
you can still ovulate
even without the monthly
that usually carries the eggs away

So where do they go, I wonder,

Imagine myself
in the Co-op
miniature eggs rolling down the produce aisle
scoop them into
a plastic bag with a twist-tie

Or belly swollen
with a few months' worth
scratch a nest
in the back corner of the yard
behind the garden

Or maybe they find their way to the sea
survive water pipes and sewers
and a little worse for wear

exchange meaningful glances
with passing codfish

Now somewhere out there
a mermaid
with my eyes

Moons

I think this child wants out.

Something about the way
my hand grips yours,
fingernails dig into your palm
so maybe you can feel what I can feel
as this child moves
centimetre by centimetre
closer to our side.

After she's joined us
and we marvel at her hair,
elbows, knees,
how little she is
yet how big,
I apologize for the crescent moons
on your hands.

You say
that's okay, really   laughing
I call them
birthmarks, amazed
at my cleverness
in this silver room.

You say

birthmarks.
They go far deeper
than anyone can see.

Delivery Room

I opened my eyes twice in there.

Once to see your face
much closer than your voice,
you are with me
on the shore, hand
stretched out,
lightly touching mine,
as the waves creep closer.

The second time to watch the head suspended
as everything
stops.
                stainless steel, polished glass, smooth stones

Eventually she gives me back to me.
She is out, and I am in
a room where joy
bounces off spit-polish shine.

I open my eyes
for good.

Swimming Lesson

They say it begins like this,
tadpoling our way into life
through silken pools of opalescent green.

We must have been pure joy
like the babies on the front page
of this morning's *Globe*—
their mothers' fingers curved round
rounded bellies
look like an extra set of ribs,
not lifelines.

I watch my daughter
front crawl toward me,
apple-round face gleams chlorine water
and accomplishment:
                    Look, Mom, I can swim now
In another part of the pool
a four-year-old boy jumps without fear
into teenage arms.

After, we share a hot fudge sundae
in a red-and-white booth at the Dairy Queen
talk about topsy tails
and:
                    Please, Mom, can't I get a
                    Barbie bride, please?

Was the light always this particular
shade of green?

When the Tooth Fairy Forgets

You wail, wake me from a dead sleep, golden loonie on my bedside table brands me FAILURE AS A MOTHER. I grab it, rush in, make you tell me how you put your hand under your pillow, instead of the coin came out with the tooth.

I say maybe the tooth fairy makes mistakes, too, forgets things like teeth and loonies and little girls who fall asleep so hopefully.

But no, you cry, she's the tooth fairy, she's beautiful and never grumpy, never late, she always knows what's for supper and dessert and she never makes her children do the dishes or make their bed, she's perfect.

Leaning over, encircling you, I say maybe she'll come tonight, and you sob, no she won't, she hates me.

I pat your pillow behind your back, say maybe you should look again, maybe the loonie slipped down behind the bed and she had a busy night, her bag was too heavy and she had to leave the tooth behind.

So you look again, doubtfully, but suddenly your face becomes a shiny round sun, your hands stretch toward me, tooth in one, loonie in the other. *See Mom, you're wrong, the tooth fairy doesn't make mistakes after all.*

Hair

A pain in the ass, the shampooing and the conditioning and the tumbleweed tangles, the combs and the brushes, elastics and scrunchies and braids, barrettes that fall out and get stepped on or lost and anything to keep it off my neck or from wrapping it round fingers all day long.

When I was two-and-a-half, my mom wrapped it in ringlets round her fingers and I remember having to lift it to pee. At ten she put me on the bus at quarter to seven with homework and hairbrush to work out the rats and at thirteen I tried out perms and curling irons and electric rollers, ripped one of my dad's old t-shirts into strips of rags that I'd twist round the lengths into knots and sleep on like a pillowful of stones.

Cleaning house I find envelopes in the bottom drawer of my grandmother's china cabinet, with dates and places of long-ago trips to the beauty parlour, or times on the stool in grandma's kitchen, tea towel draped round shivering shoulders, head bent forward not daring to breathe. I tuck in beside them the envelopes I've kept for my kids. And seeing in the sink long strands of copper and brown, I know I'm into motherhood for the long haul.

But it's that barest of moments at the end of the day, when I've washed my face and unbuttoned my shirt, taken out the clips and let it fall free, like a whisper in the night it sweeps across my shoulders—and I once again believe in possibility.

Since I'm 37

and my children tell me my hair's got more grey in it than grandma's and her body is the one I see in the mirror every morning when I get up, and I find myself going through roll call when I try to speak to my kids and I need to turn on my computer to tell me what day it is—

I guess it's only right if I can't remember the little cakes I baked for my sister's softball team that I coached when she was eight and I was sixteen and that I wrote their names on all of them (but she does)

or asking some fellow at a party if he wanted to just leave it all behind and run away with me (but he does)

or a friend's going-away party where we signed our names (even my baby daughter's) on scraps of fabric and then her friend quilted them all together and she takes it with her whenever she goes on the road

or the last time someone other than my mother or my children said I love you.

Sculpture

I wish I'd been the one
to write the lines upon your face
the stories that lie between
the ones I'll never know
you tease me about my age
how I was in diapers
while you grappled
with Sandra something-or-other
in the back seat of your father's car
                            I laugh
smooth your forehead with my fingers
delight in this new-found power
to sculpt lines out of flesh
scatter seed pearls across a page
you touch my face
bring out lines
I never knew I had

Either/Or

When you have only a short time
and a choice must be made
which will come first
loving
or supper
I know which one I'd take—

if I have to be left
I'd rather it be
washing the dishes
than lying in bed
alone

Wanted Words

You asked about my family.
Here. I have a picture.

This is my first daughter.
This is my second daughter.
They have different last names.
Ten years and three months, two fathers, apart.

This is my second daughter.
This is her [wanted word that means] brother.
They have different last names.
Ten years and five months, two mothers, apart.

This is my [wanted word that means] second daughter's brother.
This is his [wanted word that means] sister.
They have different last names.
Four years and seven months, two fathers, apart.

This is the [wanted word that means] first daughter of my second ex's new wife.
This is my first daughter.
They have the same birthday and different last names.
Exactly ten years, two fathers, two mothers, apart.

They make a [wanted word that means] family.

Sometimes When I Sleep

My ghost is not
a malevolent ghost.
It's not particular to this house
or that city—
It follows me around
like a glow follows light
visits early in the night
when walls are thinnest
It slides through and wills me
wake up

My ghost takes various
forms, sometimes spiders sometimes
snake sliding down double
helix lamp that's supposed to be
in the living room, instead
is suspended just to the left
above my head, other
times it hovers over me or
just to the right of
me and I wake, say
who are you? reach out
past it, turn on the light
but it slips into the shadow
space between the wall and
the light and
is gone

Lately I've grown used to it
miss it when it isn't here
but like that trick with light
when you look right at it
it vanishes
and when you're not looking
it's just
        there
And I say *oh, it's only you*
echoes
oh, it's only you too—

We Have Fallen

    (after Yeats)

We have fallen in the dreams
the still living leave behind
like tattered crow rags
orphaned on the line

Once in a while we'll remember,
like fog that floats
on the lowest point of land
tendrils will seep into our sleep
and maybe we'll notice
and maybe we won't,
a gnawing on the arm
of forgetting's firm grasp.

What happens when they accumulate,
these dreams?

Will they compost in our consciousness?
Will the fumes awaken new ones?

Or will they burn off
to mingle in the cumulus,
cloud our vision, colour it grey,
and tomorrow on the way to work
we'll remark:
the weatherman sure got that wrong
again.

Willow

Your roots go deep, but not deep enough to reach the river where I picture you splayed slippery on the bank's muddy edge, branches a crazy quilt weave of limbs, leaf tips trailing like a child's fingers over the side of a boat or a woman washing her hair.

Instead you're here in this barren field, yellowy leaves with spotted underbellies tired in sun that etches fissures into your bark, skin a crusty scab.

Blink, I look again. Your knots wink as finger-thin branches beckon me in.

Drawn to your shade, I nestle in the whale's-eye hollow at your base, welcome your cool canopy, live branches like the ribs of an umbrella overhead, dead ones stiff as Medusa's snakes turned to stone.

My skin wakens to the crunch of your dead fallen leaves, urged to life with air currents that play me along. Veined leaves tributaried as the insides of my eyelids, I fill my hands with them and slide them down, down, between my fingers, my tongue, leave traces of my oils, close my eyes and imagine growing into you on your riverbank, your leaf whisper *later* the only sound I hear.

Feet

Had a dream the other night
Cut off my feet mid-shin
Changed them round
the way they were supposed to go

Not the first time either
maybe the third or fourth
like rotating tires on the car
or switching socks so the big toe
won't poke through
(though it always always does)

Had some problems this time though—
Feet didn't quite fit
loose where they attached to the stumps
squished when I walked
like wet socks in boots
three sizes too big

At least I got the toes pointing in
this time—

You're gonna meet a bear
my grandfather always said
when I had my shoes on
wrong

One by One
(for Claire)

I.

Let's get this straight:
my friend did not die,
did not fall like the chestnut
that dropped from the neighbour's tree
and cracked my window pane.

Night before her second surgery
we go to visit,
one by one
we stack like cordwood
on chairs, the floor,
backs snugged to walls,
knees cradled in arms.

We tell stories
of children and work,
Liam Neeson on the cover of *George*,
how on earth could half the book club
hate *Random Passage?*
upcoming summer holidays.

Find ourselves
unable to leave,
even when the nurse eyes the corkscrew
and smells the garlic on the pizza
we've smuggled in. But finally

It's time.
One by one
we leave her.
Cocooned in our stories
we sleep.

Next morning in our offices
our phone lights greet us.
Know that right now she's sunk under anaesthetic,
know that right now they're taking her breast.
But right now it's her voice: *Thank you.*
We find out later she'd called each of us,
one by one,
to do the same.

II.

We offer to shave our heads for her
but she won't let us.
So we buy her silk scarves and fishing hats,
take turns having our pictures taken
wearing her wig.
She laughs at the injustice:
after losing all her hair
she still has to shave her legs.

III.

She tells us of the time she fell apart:
finding her crying, her doctor tries his best to soothe.
Talks about reconstruction and implants,
finally in desperation calls one of us to come.
She sobs.
It's Father's Day.
How can I take my children shopping
to buy him a present?

IV.

I can't believe it.
I lost my breast.
Eight hundred dollars,
and I can't find it anywhere.
Last time this happened
it was under the blankets at the bottom of my bed.
I've checked the laundry basket, all my drawers.
I've had to resort to foam.

Six weeks later
we ask her,
Did you ever find your breast?

Yes.

Looking for her son's birthday gift
she finds the skateboard
and the breast
behind the vacuum cleaner
in the upstairs linen closet.

V.

Another close call.
At the beach
her daughter:
Bet you can't do this, Mom.

Somersaults, backflips, til coming up for air
she looks down. Gets that feeling
like when you put dry shorts over a wet bathing suit.
Horror on both their faces: no breast.

Frantic, they dive, come up empty-handed
every time.

Til this little old lady from two cottages over yells,
Dear, are you missing something?
Holds it up for the whole beach to see.
Did you know it floats?

VI.

Question from her daughter:
Mom,
does this mean
it'll get me, too?

For Linda

I.

Lying alone I see their shape
back-lit by the night light in the hall
tantalized by their curve I feel them silk-smooth heavy
forbidden like the glass paperweight that fit my palm so perfectly
when my mother wasn't looking

nipples become firm brown berries
feel lips encircling
fingers twirling
like two dials on the radio
direct line to that space inside that holds my poems, my babies, my music,
my joy
seven years since they felt an infant's insistent tug, yet
they tingle when I hear a newborn cry

early detection, one in nine
I know I should know about self-exams
pick up a brochure at the drugstore
bury it under books and papers beside my bed
look for a lover who will learn to map
the contours of those inner walls
who will not hesitate to taste the droplets
that form unbidden

on the back page of the Books Section
in last Saturday's *Globe*
is a photograph
a woman's face and torso
naked to the sun and the joy of being alive
both arms flung back
but only one breast
where the other was
a tattoo

I long to see it up close
picture a long green stem twining its way down and across
dripping hollyhocks and roses
within each perfect bud
a tiny white bead

II.

Outside church
Linda sets me straight.

She tells me it's been ten years
since she had both of them off.
Now she drives others to chemo
Listens, counsels, rages, loves

She remembers as a child
when voices crept through walls
like cold fingers up her spine
cross shoulders, neck

when she had to escape

she'd dance shadows across the lawn
pirouette and twirl faster and faster
arms embracing arms encircling
face raised to the sun or the rain or
whatever God gave her—

Don't you see?
Now that they're both gone,
I am what I always wanted to be: ballerina

Eleanor's Eyes

She'd have a fit if she knew I was writing about her. About the egg and ham salad sandwiches, the coconut cream pie that the cat licked in the box on the table—*have another sandwich, dear. Shut up, dog, you've already had four. Good thing we were having sandwiches, if I'd cooked you supper I'd have thrown it out. That's what happens when you come late.*

Fierce guard of privacy she'd rather talk of ideas than herself. Poets she hears on the radio, politicians who won't pave her road. And Eleanor. Eleanor who would have stopped her last Sunday from talking to those journalists, Eleanor who lived with her for fifty years, the last fifteen of them blind, Eleanor who loved classical music and cats and her, Eleanor who died last Christmas.

Her paintings hang on crooked walls, cats with crazed eyes, forests with trees that sway to Eleanor's music, colours dance til she traps them with the sharp tongue of her knife, edges not so subtle blend to sunset

and time for a walk to the headland where Eleanor went every day, shows us where she scattered Eleanor's ashes across the point, ashes that left Michaelmas daisies in their wake, tiny purple stars that wink at the lobster boat slicing in front of the sun as it dangles, day's hold tenuous as it shivers then slips behind the line that marks the edge of the sea, the last boat silent, glides home.

Back inside her house I feel like I've grown to fill my skin. Beside her I'm six feet tall, music sings in my veins. Think how we shouldn't be afraid of heights, just edges.

If I Could Draw

there'd be a lot of the picture that wouldn't make it in—

To the left black dark
paints over the lighthouse
whose orange glow washes into the frame
over the top half just below the stars.

To the right the path
we've danced our way down,
rain shimmers delicate on laughing faces.
At the other end you can't see the party we've fled
where the men are drinking themselves comatose.

Just below the bottom rocks we scramble over
toes grope for soft sand,
piles of each other's clothes—
jeans sweatshirts towels
become shadows that melt to sandstone to rock.

Beneath the September sea you can't see the claws
of seaweed, can't stop as we squeal and yell, insistent
fingers grab ankles, knees, thighs, but
there's the end, the line of clear water just up ahead—
we keep going, shrieking
with the ice cold and hot blood of

seven women, who've made it and who we are
is beyond the scope of any picture
motherswivesfriendsloverssistersdaughterscreators
our white forms joining hands
every one of us beautiful as
seven moons dancing on waves one by one we sink
below the horizon singing laughing chanting
she changes everything she touches and
everything she touches changes.

Accordion cut-out where the paper's folded fourteen times,
cut the shapes
and open them, linked by more than
blood, memory, voices, water
across the sea other women join hands
and we shout to them
behind the picture they shout back
something only we and the orange stars can hear.

Choir

My friend Claire says I should get extra points for going to church when I don't have to. I tell her I'm here for the music.

Holy days of obligation and I'm here and she's not, singing my guts out losing my voice in the starburst of notes that rain down on our heads, knowing if I believed in God it'd probably be a Catholic one since they sure know how to sing. Echoes of those early years when every Sunday my grandmother stole me from my Anglican mother so maybe my soul would have a chance of being saved. I don't remember that but I do remember being nine and going to church with my best friend Shannon, not daring to eat their bread because *He would know.*

Now I don't kneel or pray, but I sing, for me and for Jack who raises his arms and pulls our voices, like he's the magnet and we the iron filings, he the moon and we the tide. He lifts his hands and ribbons of white flow through elbowtips and fingertips from somewhere just the other side of vision holding us taut like fishing line strung long, humming with the force of possibility or that urge to life some call God, when all pieces click into place and for a moment you glimpse the breadth of the universe, and things like income tax and what to get the kids for supper are just an infinitesimal part of the weave that holds us tight.

Then just as suddenly he lets us go, and we laugh at our mistakes that he says keep us humble, gifts from the angel-in-charge-of-things-as-they-really-are, say see you next time, and know the words don't matter because we're here for the music.

Sleeping

Northern lights dance us down the Western Road, to the town where we pull in to see him, warm and still beneath the thin blue sheet. It's Tuesday and he's been sleeping since Sunday, first in the room with the brown locker in the corner and the clock at the foot of the bed, the room in which his wife died eight years ago. Then later in the soft room with the flowers and the rocking chair, where we sit and watch him sleeping, curled beneath the thin blue sheet, and I wonder where he could have gotten to, and the tears won't stop.

It's the figs I see squeezed between his fingers fat with the sunshine of someone else's garden, and the crib board he pegs with such ferociousness he skunks me one more time while you snore on the couch in the kitchen (something about that couch that makes a son want to climb right in). Home-made beer in the tupperware measuring cup which he drinks from the side. The ring-toss game made with quart sealers positioned just so in front of his chair. Later we admire his sweet peas that climb the side of the house, the carefully pruned apple tree with the ladder resting against its trunk, the rows between the tomato plants swept clean like a carpet.

Another time he was sleeping but he wakened when you squeezed his foot, ever so gentle. He was confused, kept asking where we'd been and where we were going, and then he just didn't wake up anymore. He is waxen in the coffin, but I do not say good-bye, leave him to the young man in the yellow slicker, May snow swirls, wind howls.

Now tonight I cannot say good-bye to you as I leave you sleeping, that space between your lower lip and chin exactly the same as his, beneath your warm blue quilt your naked body a question mark.

What the Apple Lady Sees

The apple lady says
sure is hard to get a good
apple these days
one that crisps your tongue
and bites you back

The apple lady says
sure is hard to get good
help these days
them kids just don't want to work any more
especially when the apples
is still attached to the tree

The apple lady says
sure is funny how them townies
drives all the way here from
the city on Saturday
buys one bag of apples
then drives all the way back home

The apple lady says
sure is hard to figure out
what all those gals from the fish plant wants
with all them apples
they walks here every day
four miles in their bare feet and sandals
picks bags and bags
then walks home
they'll be back again tomorrow for more

*

The fish plant ladies say
sure is hard to fill a belly these days
when you're making three bucks an hour
after the fish plant takes room and board
for a bed in a bunkhouse
fish guts and blood puddles
congealing out the back door

The fish plant ladies say
we've cleaned out the Sally Ann
for the second time this week
shoes and sweaters and snowsuits
towels and blankets and booties
just so our babies
can keep warm

The fish plant ladies say
there's more to hunger
than belly hunger
when you're half a world away
from the ones who love you
baby on a breast
no substitute for the man
you've left behind

skin hunger
body hunger
soul hunger
that space inside
that apples won't fill
no matter how many bags
you drag home

Dust

In the time it takes
for a baby's first cry

I pick up the pieces of me
that fall between us
casually slip them into my bag
sweep their dust off the bar
into my hand
and blow

It mingles with the smoke
that clings to your hair, your skin
the clothes your wife
will hang on the line
to air

and next summer
you'll wonder why your geraniums grew so well
especially the red ones

On Learning Someone You Know Is Having an Affair

She's moved off the farm
Taken the kids and the furniture
says she'll never go back
even if he comes to his senses
and drops that slut

Why, she's young enough to be his daughter
I nod, understanding
Mid-life crisis, maybe?
They seem to be happening younger these days

I think about my sixteenth summer
A friend
kissing me behind the gym
on our way home from soccer one night

But my boyfriend kissed better
so that was the end of that

Now wish it was that simple
as I kiss you good-bye
say have a nice day
drop kids at daycare
and fleetingly wonder
how far I can get on
half a tank of gas
and an Irving credit card

Seven-year-itch

Seven-year-itch
HA!
try bludgeon
   dull razor
   slow burn

Sometimes the silent treatment
for days
wondering what I did wrong
this time

Or one-sided arguments
(He always liked the sound of his voice)
You're not your mother
I'm not your father
When will you grow up?

Always harping
you should read more
don't make so much noise when you eat
stop being cute
stand up for yourself

Finally I did
Shed seven years
layers of old skin
Blew the dust off
till I shone
Mornings
wake up, think
I must leave
then remember—
I already did

Cold Feet

I still remember how a slow kiss ignites the fuse
fuels the heat that makes me forget
all about
cold feet.

I need warm feet to sleep
and since it's only me in the bed
those'd be mine.

Invariably find myself under covers
fishing for socks I've peeled off
in the dead of night, or, if I'm really lazy
snagging them with a toe and hauling them up
far enough to grab hold of
and pull on.

Sometimes lose them altogether,
drag myself out of bed to get more, later
find them tucked damp in the corners of sheets
fresh from the line.

My ex quizzes me if I'm seeing anyone
(one of those four-times-a-year lunches
he takes all his exes to)
says it shows a singular lack of imagination.

I say whose?

A Threat or a Promise?

Always the smart ass
he could flirt with the best of them.
Plaid shirt with the domes
he'd undo in one move,
size 30 Levis worn white at the knees,
the handtooled leather belt with the Caterpillar belt buckle,
string tie for weddings,
and always the cowboy boots,
at 30 above or below
(I got the boots, my sister the tie,
no one wanted the belt)

One drink made him sociable, two obnoxious,
knowing young the right time to ask for
quarters and puppies
(she still calls our dog his $200 drunk,
plus the price of getting drunk)

And at three, knowing how
to make ourselves scarce—
Is that a threat or a promise?
his favourite line.

Like I said today when you asked if you could trade
a poem for a hug
February in the longest winter of my heart
and I sure could use a poem right now
not to mention the hug

The promise of a man who jumps sideways to conclusions
The threat of a man and his January thaw

I see those boots stashed
upstairs in my closet
your waiting feet
a perfect size 8

"Boys Like Girls Whose Hair Outweighs Their Brain"
—Ana Graham, "Why Play Dumb?" (*Globe & Mail*, March 4, 2006)

Sweet sixteen and bad boys
sugar my tongue
riding in cars leaves me
with road rash lips
tumbleweed hair
back seat tattoos
crisscrossed on my back

A glance that starts at the ball field
ends in the backroom stacks
of the hometown rag
ink tendrils my nostrils
dust papers my skin
as lips chase leads
under my white India cotton blouse

by day Mozart
waltzes patterned proofs inside my head
metaphored schematics clutter margins and notebooks
and labyrinth scores run background noise

by night
field spin spills brain cells on grass
Lonesome Charlie and Baby Duck swing me by my braids
stars circle dangerously close to my horizon
as boys and cars and theorems
and planets and moons
track in and out of orbit

Boys presaged chaos theory
bumping trays in the cafeteria
led to hot September schoolyards
breezes waving through leaves in the trees above
as hands sculpted waves below

Boys danced me through high school
and university
the trick to let them believe they were leading
as my toes purpled and knees bruised
and I grew my hair to my waist

Later I learned to sleep
with boys who were almost smarter than me
and never with ones who had wives
I liked

Boys at the library
boys in the grocery store
boys beside me at the meeting table
their thighs tanned golden
smooth as an oaken banister
burnished by my palm

boys who have no fear
who won't look away when eyes collide
brush my shoulder with their fingertips
drift my hair back from my cheek
and whisper in my ear
the car's outside

boys who will
knife-dive off an edge
into a still pond with me
the slightest of ripples
as we slit open the water
fin our way down
til all sound recedes
but heartbeats

I breaststroke my way
back up
alone

wipe the droplets from my face
squeeze rivers from the strands of hair between my fingers
taut as a violin bow strung heavy with music

take the scissors
cut it
off

So, gifted girl-child
you keep your hair short
right from the start
and know those boys
don't stand a chance

Eight and Counting

On the other side of the glass
three-legged Coda
reconnoitres

she does not glide smooth through grass
stalking downy woodpeckers
who hover at the suet in the magnolia tree

nor does she manoeuvre through hills
like the Gagetown soldiers
preparing for Afghanistan or Iraq
just out of sight
behind the fence
that runs the road to Fredericton

rather
three-legged Coda
plays Russian Roulette with her name
awkward as a tall man on stilts
clumsy as magnolia branches in a windstorm
determined to push beyond the glass
stretch the edges of her fields
under a bruised sky

thumbing her tail at a world
that eats lambs and *Shih Tzus* and Pomeranians
and legs of cats that one time
forget to come in
after dark

Blue Moon

On this blue moon New Year's Eve
I realize

You called me
on the first full moon in December

But I wasn't there

Instead
two shadows walked me home
one from the streetlight
and one from the moonlight
so round and full and ready to burst
it lit up the sky
like a miner's headlamp searching for
that elusive vein of gold

Startled
I looked for someone
behind me
beside me

but it was only me
and your call waiting

Out of Wedlock

I am
all out, I mean,
of luck
in love, and marriage,
though (thankfully) not children
(though they were out, too)
but not from lack of proposals
just none I wished to accept

Hell hath no fury...
and then some, I say,
as you ask to make
an *honest woman* of me

So you want honest
You, the man who believes
that a bird in the hand is only good
if there are two more
in the bushes
sheathed in silken promises
and a little footsie on the side

Okay, let me be honest
even if I were sleeping with you
out of wedlock
—which I'm not, lucky that—
the term honest woman
means my children are either lies or half-truths
or the state of sleeping with someone I once loved
the same

I'm already honest
too honest
for you

So if I say
you run like a girl
it will be a compliment
so I'll just say
run.

Living at Sea Level

The Language of Seashells
(for Pete Hay)

I know seashells, you say,
as you walk Nebraska Beach
head down, hands behind back

The vernacular names, anyway
painted ladies, flower cones, doughboys
cart-ruts, hairy arks

It was simple, you say,
I'd pick up something beautiful
and want to know what it was

A man who knows his place
on an island off an island
at the edge of the end of the world

Where the sea writes its story
on dolerite and mudstone
revealing the lines and the distances
between blood and carbon, breathing and not

Where the absences make you ache
and you're forever reminded of them
as you walk the bush or shore

Where the tragedy, you say,
is not that our young people leave,
but that they don't come back

Just up ahead you catch movement on the cliff
a blackfella? a chinaman?
a thylacine? a child?

But it is only the light
a reminder of what's missing
and what's here

Back from the beach
you add a chinaman's fingernail to your shelf
brush off the grit of a thousand years of waves
on rock and bone and glass and shell

Out the corner of your eye
the glimpse you carry
like sand trapped in the seams of your pockets

Living at Sea Level

i. Colouring in the lines

Born without the ocean at my feet,
this living at sea level scares me.

I am used to thin air,
wraparound sky so close you
scrape it with your fingernail, jagged
peaks on the horizon my comfort zone, narrowing
my view.

My friend Libby sees a mountain
and is compelled to climb it,
just to see what's on the other side.
I see a mountain and I soar on the updraft
swoop on the down
til I'm smack in the middle
of the palm of the valley
where dawn takes longer to get to
and day is quicker to leave.

There the edges are blurred,
not knowing
where your land ends and
mine begins.

Here, at sea level, it's pruned and edged
steadfast and bound by
a prairie of ocean,
limits constant, inevitable.

But it is only here, colouring in the lines
that bind me to this place
that my edges are defined.

I'm getting used to sleeping
with the roar of the ocean in my ears.

ii. In my dream

I'm on top of Tea Hill
breath-holding
gravity-defying
place
where stomach flips
holds
and lands

and I'm on my way down again
to see Northumberland Strait
a fuzzy bathmat
at the base of the hill
blue shimmers through the miasma
of an August noon

my daughters are with me
eight and four, young enough
to wear
(without complaint)
the matching dresses
I've sewn for them, cotton print
lacy cuffs and collars
Victorian dolls tumbling through
daisies, Indian paintbrush, clover

eyes random
follow them as they bend
to pick a strawberry, careen
to catch a butterfly, snag
something in my
peripheral vision

slow motion turn
and the water's gone

past Governor's Island,
Squaw Point, Earnscliffe, Point Prim,
red snakes the shore,
bones of boat ribs
lumps of sandstone
fish flop in clear focus
though they're miles away

if I don't wake up first
I know what's going to happen next
because it always does:

we're in the car
racing, racing
for Strathgartney
second-highest point of land
with the North River causeway
at sea level to cross
and even if we make it
I know we don't have a chance in hell
at four hundred and fifty feet

when all that water
comes rushing back in

iii. First story of arrival

Serendipity and warm winds blow me here a
western Canada nomad
looking for a place to set down roots

where land meets ocean meets sky
on an early evening in June
light otherworldly
sharpens edges like beach grass on
cliffs, lupins, dunes

I skim across a glassened strait
overwhelmed by this sense of home

from the inside out
the Island takes me in

iv. Alternate story of arrival

I'm flotsam in the Strait
cast adrift
belly empty, lips sandpaper, heart in shreds
Prince Edward Island floats just ahead
red cliff teeth
sluice grass throat
back paddle frantic
but the tide is too strong
I succumb to its pull
am washed up naked on its
red-sand tongue

taken
from the outside in

v. That second morning

Fog
pillows fifty shades of white
redolent with fish and salt and creosote
heavy in my lungs

in this bubble
I drive along the TransCanada
from time to time catch a glimpse of
green field, red road
a marsh slipping by, spreading
to the flat silver back of ocean
and just as quickly
gone

Strathgartney Hill and I'm above the fog
sightline down the West River clean
to the Northumberland Strait
between mounds of hills
with their fifty shades of green
as the sun lights on trees
I see a look-off at the side of the road
but don't take the time to stop
twenty-two years later
regret tastes like fog rolling over my tongue

vi. Palm reading

I hold the Island in the palm of my hand
my story a lifeline stitched into the loam like
rippled sand patterns
on waved-carved dunes
my love line the
    zigs
and
        zags
of potato drills
new-mown hay
stripes
of red and yellow
and always the green

clapboard walls
plumb-lined roofs
mounds of hills, lawns and fields edged
by fences, curbs
stippled with lupins and phlox and Queen Anne's lace

patches sewn together with hedgerows
bumping up against a cloak of blue
fabric a whorl and eddy, capped in white

wide angle lens narrows
palm lines deepen with my staying

vii. Wind from away

When the hurricane came calling
it battered the door
raged against roof, windows, fences, walls
but stoic we aligned ourselves
centuries of weathering storms
pooled in our blood

but oak and spruce and pine don't stand a chance
against tropical winds
intended for coral reef breakwaters
and palms with elastic spines

leaves in late summer fullness
green sails drag their masts to ground
windrows hold the patches together
stitch-rip
century-old roots
that should have held fast
only a shallow tangle in the cling of red clods

what was it like
I wonder
in that last explosion as you hit the ground
a dawning
that you're not as rooted
as you think you are

viii. Beachcombing

we've spent the afternoon
lazy in the heat
combing the shore for beachglass
(blue the holy grail now that Noxzema started using plastic)
7-Up greens
beer bottle browns
frosty whites
become windows
two clamshells round oversized doors
and driftwood bendy bridges over
moats afloat with marram grass
we've pulled from the dunes behind us

salt-lick-white skin shivers
as the golden hairs of your thigh
touch mine

now
golden Brackley Beach
ball floats on the horizon just out of reach
toes numb
as the light catches
in this in-
between place
of land and sea
froth bubbles my toes
seaweed cloys my ankles
sand wraps round my feet
and I sink to my knees

if I don't move soon
I'll be here forever
(*don't move*)

Biding Your Time

You sing your way to me
winter Saturday killing-time-before-the-Market morning
your voice raw ragged round the edges

Gene MacLellan's "Bidin' my Time"
the one you learned for a concert in Bonshaw in the fall
put together by an old love
(you didn't know that then)

Your voice a balm for the heart-that-knows-it's-leaving
Gene's words a poem breaking the heart-that-wants-to-stay
the glow from last night's wine elixir as I reach to touch the hand
of the man-my-island-has-given-me to make sure that I'll come back

I will wait for you, you whisper

bide your time
while the strands of your voice
anchor me to home

Acknowledgements

Many of these poems—or versions thereof—have appeared in the chapbook *Scars* (Saturday Morning Chapbooks, 2004), anthologies *The New Poets of Prince Edward Island* (Ragweed, 1995) and *Landmarks: An Anthology of New Atlantic Canadian Poetry of the Land* (Acorn, 2001), and journals *Contemporary Verse 2, Famous Reporter, Island, Vintage 98-99, Arts East,* and *blueshift*. "Boys Like Girls Whose Hair Outweighs Their Brain" was written for and presented as part of CBC Radio's Poetry Face-off.

Thanks to all the writers, workshop leaders, and friends who have read through my manuscript at one time or another and offered editorial suggestions. One of the challenges of taking this long to publish a book is that if I try to name them, I'll leave someone out. I can only console myself by saying: *You know who you are.*

Thanks go to my writing groups who have been such an integral and cherished part of my writing journey: the Ladies Auxiliary and the WWW (Wild Women Writers, or whatever it is "W" stands for on any given day...).

Thanks to Dave Godfrey, Libby Oughton, Richard Lemm, Frank Ledwell, Harry Baglole, and Pete Hay, who have played pivotal roles in my publishing, poetry, and island studies realms. Thanks to Terrilee Bulger, who is taking the new Acorn Press to the next stage; Matt Reid, who is turning my poems into something beautiful to hold; Jane Ledwell, whose editorial artistry is legend on Prince Edward Island (and I finally got to experience it first-hand!); and Pamela Swainson, who hears the music, too.

Thanks to my family and friends, who gave me the stories, and to Dad's oldest sister, my Auntie Jean, whose wise words during first-year university, "You can only do as good as you can do," have followed me from island to island. Thanks to Mike for the harmony. And, finally, to my favourite young women in the whole wide world: I'm so proud to be known as Heather and Mikhala's mom.